Performance Driven Journal

PERFORMANCE DRIVEN JOURNAL™

THE PLAYBOOK TO SCRIPT A WINNING ATTITUDE IN LIFE, LEADERSHIP AND BUSINESS

DAVID L. HANCOCK
BOBBY KIPPER

NEW YORK

LONDON • NASHVILLE • MELBOURNE • VANCOUVER

Performance Driven Journal

The Playbook to Script a Winning Attitude in Life, Leadership and Business

Published in New York, New York, by Morgan James Publishing. Morgan James is a trademark of Morgan James, LLC. www.MorganJamesPublishing.com

Morgan James
BOGO™

A **FREE** ebook edition is available for you
or a friend with the purchase of this print book.

CLEARLY SIGN YOUR NAME ABOVE

Instructions to claim your free ebook edition:
1. Visit MorganJamesBOGO.com
2. Sign your name CLEARLY in the space above
3. Complete the form and submit a photo
   of this entire page
4. You or your friend can download the ebook
   to your preferred device

ISBN 9781631954474 paperback
ISBN 9781631954481 eBook

Cover Design by:
Brittany Bondar
makeyourmarkdesign.com

Interior Design by:
Christopher Kirk
www.GFSstudio.com

Morgan James is a proud partner of Habitat for Humanity Peninsula
and Greater Williamsburg. Partners in building since 2006.

Get involved today! Visit
MorganJamesPublishing.com/giving-back

Dedicated to the performers who read this journal and use it!

TABLE OF CONTENTS

ACKNOWLEDGMENTS

As we continue on our journey of performance, we realize that without the help of top performers, this dream would not have become a reality. We would sincerely like to express our great appreciation to the following individuals for their valued support and Performance-Driven attitude in helping us bring this project to completion:

Jim Howard, our publisher

Margo Toulouse, our managing editor

Amanda Rooker, our editor

Brittany Bondar, for our cover concept and branding

Chris Treccani, for our cover, interior design, and layout

Bethany Marshall, who pitches us to the bookstores

Amber Parrott, Taylor Chaffer, Lauren Howard, Heidi Nickerson, and Jessica Moran, our author support, marketing, and publicity team

Paul Edwards, our esteemed wordsmith

We would also both like to thank our families and individual friends who throughout our lives have enabled us to pursue the performance of a lifetime.

Most importantly, we want to thank those who read this journal and use it.

INTRODUCTION

As we wrote in our previous book, *Performance-Driven Thinking*, we realize that almost everyone has the desire to perform. Some may even know that they were born to perform. But that's not enough. There has to be a conscious *decision* to perform.

Even the best-trained athletes have to have the thought that translates to the will to perform. How many times have you heard the statement "They just didn't show up tonight" when describing a team that suffered a huge loss? Does this mean that they were not physically present? Of course not. They were there in body, but not in thought. They did not leave behind their ability to perform; they left behind their will to perform.

Sports stars, musicians, great actors, and other successful people do not perform by accident. Inevitably they have the stamina of thought *and* will to push through the tough process that eventually will lead them to peak performance on the world's biggest stages, whatever their fields may be. It comes down to their ability to know what they want and to have the mental strength to go for it.

Performance doesn't depend solely on the desire to succeed, and it doesn't depend solely on the effort or will to succeed. The two needed to be connected through a particular thought process. We have defined this process as Performance-Driven Thinking, and we think it could change your life!

Here is our definition of Performance-Driven Thinking:

> **Performance-Driven Thinking**: The thought process that connects the desire to perform with the will to perform a specific task or goal.
> **desire**: to long or hope for something you want
> **will**: to decide, attempt, or bring desire to action

This definition is based not merely on research but on reality. You can't begin to perform until you make a conscious decision to do so. But we want to do more than simply define Performance-Driven Thinking. It truly is our desire to bring it out in you! We don't want you to waste another day without stepping up to the plate. We don't want you to continue to go through life wondering what could have been if you had only taken that next step. No matter how big or small, your next step could be the one that changes your life.

If we want to raise the level of performance in our people and ourselves, we need more than simply coaching or encouragement. We need to understand what is missing in our *thinking* so we can plug in what is needed. That's exactly what you will implement in this Performance-Thinking Journal.

Performance-Driven Thinking: The Goal Is the Journey

First of all, congratulations on even considering becoming a Performance-Driven Thinker in a new, rapidly changing world. It's challenging, but you're in for a lot of fun. Work? Of course, lots of work, but fun too. Lots of fun, if you do it right.

The first thing you'll notice about being a Performance-Driven Thinker is that your goals will be different from the old-fashioned goals of a non-Performance-Driven Thinker. If you're an entrepreneur or a business owner, for example, a Performance-Driven Enterprise is flexible, innovative, unconventional, low in overhead costs, dependent, interactive, generous, enjoyable, and profitable. The goal of the enterprise is to stay that way.

Look at the entrepreneurs all around you. If you can't see many, it's because they are not Performance-Driven Thinkers. Instead they're buried in work, rarely coming up for the fresh air of free time. When you learn to truly perform, you become far more efficient and effective. In fact, the goals of Performance-Driven Thinkers allow them the freedom to pursue interests beyond work—while amassing an income beyond that of their workaholic ancestors.

You can always tell Performance-Driven Thinkers by their goals. They are not as money minded as the entrepreneurs who came before them. They seem to be happier with the work that they're doing and appear to care like crazy about satisfying the needs of their customers. You've never seen follow-up done the way these people do it. They stay in touch constantly with their customers. It's not as if they are working at their business, but rather demonstrating passion for their work. Their goal is to express that passion with excellence and transform it into profits.

Not surprisingly, Performance-Driven Thinkers achieve their goals on a daily basis. Their long-term goals are lofty. Those goals exist in the future. Their short-term goals are even loftier. Those exist in the present, for that is the domain of the Performance-Driven Thinker. That is where her goals are to be found in abundance.

Your ability to plan for the future and learn from the past will determine your level of comfort in the present, in the here and now. Being a Performance-Driven Thinker means realizing that these can be the good old days and that you don't have to wait for the joy that comes with success. It's there in front of you, in the present moment.

Wake up from the Old American Dream and realize that it has changed for the better—the New American Dream is more achievable, more enjoyable, and much healthier than the old one.

Although at this moment you may find the New American Dream unconventional, as all Performance-Driven endeavors are, you'll soon see that it will come to be the mainstream American Dream, because it is achievable and brings increased benefits. Most of us can dream it and then delight in making it come true.

Originally, the dream meant having enough food and protection from the weather. Cave dwellers dreamt of hunting enough game or gathering an abundance of nuts and berries. That dream has changed, replaced by the hope of earning enough money to feed a hungry family. The Industrial Revolution took care of that and eventually gave birth to the American Dream: a house, a job, and financial security.

Entrepreneurs of the twentieth century were motivated by a slightly different version of the American Dream. In place of a house, a job, and financial security, they sought fortune, security, expansion, and power. But that journey was characterized by workaholism, sacrifice, and greed.

The entrepreneur of the future will need to be a Performance-Driven Thinker—one who thrives on the non-traditional, does the unconventional if the conventional is non-sensical, and knows that working in the new millennium requires rethinking the nature of being a successful entrepreneur.

The performance goals of the twentieth-century entrepreneur were simple—securing a job, a family, a home. The goals of the Performance-Driven Thinker are considerably loftier than those of the past: attaining work that is satisfying, enough money to enjoy freedom from worry about it, health good enough to take for granted, a family or bonding with others where you can give and receive love and support, fun that does not have to be pursued but exists in daily living, and the longevity to appreciate with wisdom that which you and those you love have achieved.

Balance will be the new dream. Performance-Driven Thinkers who go about creating a profit-producing enterprise will begin with balance, actually starting with work that makes them happy, the goal of all Performance-Driven dreams. Once that has been attained, Performance-Driven Thinkers will be able to pursue their other goals: making money, enjoying free time, maintaining health, and having fun.

Most important, as we hope you realize, the goal of the Performance-Driven Thinker is the journey itself.

Chapter 1

You Were Born to Perform

Why do some people take the stage in life, while others hesitate? That is the magic question that faces our entire society. Parents wonder why some children perform and others hold back. Educators are equally perplexed, spending countless hours (and dollars) trying to motivate performance in students. And despite the myriad of books and systems guaranteeing better performance and productivity, most businesses still struggle to find the right formula that works long term. While most of our programming and efforts in the past several years have focused on group or team performance, one central issue still remains. We cannot escape the fact that performance (or lack thereof) is fundamentally an individual decision.

David L. Hancock & Bobby Kipper

Start with Status Quo—But Don't Stay There!

Without pointing fingers or getting judgmental, we're going to observe the people around us to get a feel for our tendency to settle for the status quo. In the space below, take note of where you see people around you—at home, at work, in your day's activities, in the news, etc.—"settle" for the status quo. Bonus points if you catch *yourself* doing it. It can look like:

- 🔄 "Feelings over Everything"—everyone gets a trophy; nobody wins or loses
- 🔄 "Radical Egalitarianism"—everyone gets paid the same regardless of effort or conduct

- ⚡ "Tall Poppy Syndrome"—contempt for people who stand out or go the extra mile
- ⚡ "Elephant in the Room"—everyone avoids confronting an obvious issue or problem
- ⚡ "The Squeaky Wheel Gets Replaced First"—keeping silent when you should speak
- ⚡ "We've always done it this way, so we'll always do it this way"—resistance to change

Notes

_____

_____

_____

_____

Desire and Will: Questions for Reflection

1. Did you notice yourself or anyone else enforce or avoid disruption of the status quo? Do you think they did so passively, or by making decisions?

_____

_____

_____

_____

2. When you observe these situations, do you notice how people can be physically present, and still not perform? Do you see how they can have an opportunity in front of them and be immobilized, because they don't know how to *think* about it?

_____

_____

_____

_____

> **Performance-Driven Thinking:** The thought process that connects *desire* to perform with the *will* to perform a specific task or goal.

3. Using this definition, which quality do you think was lacking *more* in the situations you observed: desire, or will?

_____

_____

_____

_____

Desire

4. Can you think of a situation in your life where you have a *desire* to perform, but lack the will? Do you want better physical shape, performance at work, or stronger relationships— but can't make it happen?

_____

_____

_____

_____

5. Have you ever felt motivated to achieve something, only to discover the path to your dream was filled with boring, repetitive work that seemed like a road to nowhere?

_____

_____

_____

Will

6. What about when you have the *will*, but not the desire? If you received a poor or mediocre grade in school, did your teacher ever say something like, "You're capable of whatever you put your mind to doing"?

_____

_____

_____

7. Without desire, willpower will not last. Have you ever set out to accomplish something, only to find yourself on a hamster wheel where the goalposts keep moving every time you get close to a goal set for you by others?

_____

_____

_____

8. Do you have a "*Not* To-Do" list, to help you eliminate things that you *can*, but should not do? Would you agree we "surrender" a lot of our lives by willingly doing things that aren't connected to our desires?

_____

_____

_____

_____

A Change in the Dream. The original "American Dream" was simply to find food and shelter. After the Industrial Revolution, it evolved into having a house, a job and financial security. After World War II, it mutated into seeking a fortune, security, expansion and power. But that collapsed at the dawn of the twenty-first century, and the internet age brought a new version. It is now our dream to find satisfying work, sufficient funds to escape freedom from financial worry, health good enough to take for granted, family or community of love and support, fun in daily living, and living long enough to appreciate it all with wisdom.

9. If you agree with all (or part) of this version of the American Dream, do you think it is likely to manifest itself automatically, or will you have to change how you think to make it a reality?

_____

_____

_____

_____

10. Do you have dreams or desires that you've thrown away or burned? Do you feel as though responsibilities like paying bills or caring for loved ones have "canceled" them?

_____

_____

_____

_____

Hopefully, these questions have you thinking and meditating on possibilities. In the next chapter, we'll tackle some big obstacles to Performance-Driven Thinking.

Chapter 2

WHEN EVERYBODY GETS A TROPHY

The important issue to grasp is that while performance is an individual choice, entitlement is an easy hiding place, especially in group settings such as offices of organizations with a number of employees. And once this sense of entitlement starts, it acts as a quick-spreading disease. What motivates an individual's work ethic outside of the will to perform? Regardless of your upbringing or other developmental circumstances, performance still comes down to a choice. That same choice drives the masses to entitlement.

David L. Hancock & Bobby Kipper

E ntitlement runs amok in modern society, and you will find it in nearly every cultural, political, and moral argument in your newsfeed. The core struggle is between performers, who understand the principle of earning rewards, and bystanders, who expect them whether or not they deserve them.

Below, write about a time when you observed or participated in circumstances where everyone got the same reward, regardless of merit.

_____

_____

_____

What did you grow up believing, concerning the equality of each person? Were you taught to believe you should receive a trophy, good grades or recognition just for showing up?

_____

_____

_____

_____

_____

What about the opposite? Did you grow up believing people aren't worth anything unless they perform and excel? Would you look down your nose at someone with less talent and experience making a sincere effort?

_____

_____

_____

_____

_____

Performance versus Entitlement: Questions for Reflection

1. When you have clear expectations for performance, you have work to do. But when there are no expectations, you don't have to do anything. Do either of these situations diminish or stop you from making a choice in how you respond?

_____

_____

_____

_____

_____

2. "Performers are *never* satisfied, but they *don't* complain. Entitlement seekers *are* satisfied (with not performing), but they *still* complain." Isn't that ironic? Why would you still complain, even if you're satisfied that all you have to do is show up?

_____

_____

_____

_____

_____

_____

_____

_____

3. Knowing these outcomes, would you rather be a performer, or an entitlement seeker? What kind of person would you rather have in your organization?

_____

_____

_____

_____

_____

_____

_____

_____

_____

Use the terms from chapter 2 to fill in the table below. This exercise is designed to trigger your thoughts that associate with how performers think and the things they do.

Entitlement	Performers
Embrace the comfort of entitlement	
Bring out complaints	
Are satisfied, but still complain	
Want to maintain status quo with current rewards	
Speak to cover up their actions	
Ignore challenges	

Rewording the Ten Dirty Lies You Must Stop Believing

1. **Time is money**. Which is easier to get back if you lose it: time, or money?

   _____

   _____

   _____

   _____

   _____

2. **Owning a business means workaholism**. If this were true, employees would be exempt from workaholism. Yet it happens to them all the time too. What's the *real* problem here?

   _____

   _____

   _____

   _____

   _____

3. **Marketing is expensive**. There are other ways to market besides paid advertising. If this is true, how do small businesses succeed?

   _____

   _____

   _____

   _____

   _____

4. **Big corporations are like wombs**. Until a recession or global crisis hits, of course. "Wombs" become "tombs" very quickly. How can you avoid the perils of poorly-run large businesses?

_____

_____

_____

_____

_____

5. **Youth is better than age**. Better-looking, perhaps. More physically energetic, definitely. But how can having no experience or wisdom possibly be better for business, a decidedly mental sport?

_____

_____

_____

_____

_____

6. **You need a job**. This would be better stated, "You need income." Where it comes from is irrelevant, so long as it's lawful and moral. Why limit your income, freedom and expression, when there are so many viable alternatives?

_____

_____

_____

_____

_____

7. **Heaven is in the afterlife**. Why, then, are we told "The kingdom of heaven is at hand?" Why would you not prefer, if you knew how, to bring heaven to earth?

8. **The purpose of education is to teach facts**. Facts are important, but they're useless if we have no passion for learning them. What do you think? Is knowledge power, or is "Knowledge + Passion = Power"?

_____

_____

_____

_____

_____

9. **Retirement is a good thing**. Maybe this is better said, "Financial independence in old age is a good thing." What do you think about the idea of working as an elder, mentor and advisor in your old age? Would you like to defy age and influence succeeding generations?

_____

_____

_____

_____

_____

10. **If you want it done right, do it yourself**. Poor teachers and leaders are known to say this. Performance-Driven Thinkers say, "Don't do anything you can properly delegate." Where do you feel like you can't trust others to do things as well as you?

_____

_____

_____

_____

_____

Your Most Loyal Companion as a Performance-Driven Thinker

Another reason it's bad for everyone to get a trophy is it conditions people away from *failure*. The paradigm shift you need to convert your mentality sees failure not only as inevitable, but equally valuable as success. Bystanders, who we'll cover in later chapters, spend their lives trying to avoid failure. Performance-Driven Thinkers embrace and learn from it.

Make a list of some of your failures, especially ones where you recall learning valuable lessons.

_____

_____

_____

_____

_____

_____

_____

Now…which of those valuable lessons would you be willing to sell, if you could, in exchange to go back to the ignorance you had at the time?

_____

_____

_____

_____

_____

_____

Things That Make Failure . . . Fail

Gone are the days where you worked at the same job in the same company for forty years and retired. British management guru Charles Handy predicted that "a career tomorrow will most likely consist of a dozen jobs on and off payrolls of large and small firms in two or three industries." The future belongs to those who can generate multiple income streams to support their lives, so that we will move from a "knowledge-based" economy to a "performance-based" model.

What Can You Perform With? Questions for Reflection

1. Where have you already invested time, money, and energy to gain working knowledge of a subject, task, or skill? How can you match it to the needs of the global marketplace?

_____

_____

_____

_____

_____

2. Where do you already have a high level of skill that's come naturally for you throughout your life? How could you apply it to benefit others and reap a reward?

_____

_____

_____

_____

3. Where have you shown a tremendous ability to perform but perhaps not used it? What do you feel stands in the way of choosing to exhibit your talent?

_____

_____

_____

_____

_____

4. America's sense of entitlement causes many of its people to move into the "slow lane" of life, hoping things will "automatically" work out well. Take another moment to observe the people who surround you daily, and (without judging) see if you can spot things they say or do that reveal a passive sense of entitlement.

_____

_____

_____

_____

_____

_____

Five Keys to Overcome Entitlement Thinking

Using the list on page 49 of *Performance-Driven Thinking*, fill in the blanks below to take your first steps on the road out of the entitlement mentality:

1. Understand your _____ and _____ performance expectations.

2. Go _____ what's expected in your role.

3. Resist _____ the crowd to "entitlement."

4. Concentrate on _____ and not the _____.

5. Use your _____, _____, and _____ to the maximum.

Now, take a few moments to write out some of the expectations you have for personal and professional performance. Ignoring what others do or how they perform, write down some ways you could use what you have to go beyond what's expected in your role.

_____

_____

_____

_____

Chapter 3

ATTITUDE

Performance comes down to connecting *desire* with the *will* to act in order to achieve. Frankly, people desire a lot of things in life, but many refuse to take action on those desires. Many people have a desire to lose excess weight, but how many will carry out the necessary action to actually experience results? In business, most people want to be successful and get to the top of their pay grade. But how many are willing to put the time in to develop the skills necessary to move to the desired level? To put it in stronger terms, most people desire to win and be successful. But many fail to connect their desire to the *will* to get the desired results. Performance-Driven Thinking is established when our wants in life are directly connected to our actions to achieve. Simply wanting without action is a wish that is unlikely to become reality.

David L. Hancock & Bobby Kipper

ow that you've practiced observing performers and bystanders, it's time to turn your gaze inward and shine light on your own inner bystander. Again, we do this without judgment, criticism, or condemnation; we're simply observing.

Negativity Is a Sign of Inner Defeat

Pause for a moment and think of relationships, circumstances, or responsibilities in your life that feel like foregone conclusions. A quarrelsome spouse, perhaps, or a tradition (like Christmas) that's supposed to be joyful . . . and you find it painful. Or a role you play where you feel unqualified to improve anything, and so you "check out" instead of engaging. Write them out in the space below.

_____

_____

_____

_____

_____

_____

Attitude: Questions for Reflection

1. When you look at these situations where you've thrown in the towel, what do you think it would feel like (or look like) to overcome them, with honor and love for all concerned?

_____

_____

_____

_____

_____

_____

2. Why do you think you have these specific blind spots and dead ends in your life? How do you interpret situations and people that seem to exist to make things difficult for you?

_____

_____

_____

_____

_____

_____

3. In an age where you can so easily access information and knowledge, and where money can buy the best talent, skills, and strength, why do you think the biggest/strongest/wealthiest/most intelligent *don't* always win?

_____

_____

_____

_____

4. Think of your favorite "underdog winner." The 1980 USA Olympic Hockey Team, for example, or Buster Douglas's 1990 knockout of Mike Tyson, who was favored 42 to 1 to win. Why do you think they won?

_____

_____

_____

_____

The 3 Biggest Obstacles to Performance-Driven Thinking

1. **Identify your opponent**. Deepen your understanding of your biggest opponents as you fill in their definitions in the table below, based on page 56 of *Performance-Driven Thinking*.

Opponent	Definition
Lack of desire	
Lack of will	
Fear of failure	
Past history	
Lack of knowledge/skills/abilities	
Lack of time or time-management skills	
Lack of resources	

2. **Preparing for opponents**. If you could be given an award for "performance-driven walking," you'd win in a landslide. You've spent a lifetime rehearsing and practicing. Take a moment to consider a performance that terrifies you. What difference do you think it would make to practice performing it for an hour per day for two to three months?

_____

_____

_____

3. **Expect to win**. Over the course of life, we make "agreements" about certain things. Some of these are completely worth making: "Gravity will make you fall, so jumping off a cliff is a bad idea." Others are terrible mistakes: "I failed the last five times I tried, so this time's not going to be any different."

The habit you need to overcome these agreements starts with taking a ruthless inventory of every little assumption or agreement you make about anything. What do you automatically think when certain things happen? Do you groan, "Here we go again," or mumble, "It's always going to be like this"? Make notes throughout your day of the thoughts you have by writing them out here.

_____

_____

_____

Once you know the lies you've swallowed and recycled, it's time to change those expectations. You might not always meet them, but you can't guarantee they won't happen if you constantly expect to fail, be defeated, or disappointed! Write down your new expectations below.

_____

_____

_____

Making the Two into One

You've just been through a straddling exercise. You addressed your lower self by acknowledging and taking responsibility for areas where you've embraced defeat. And you started replacing those beliefs with those of your higher self, your new performance-driven expectations.

Just as you can't embrace one without the other, so you must now break the old division between work and leisure. It's time to put work in its proper place, integrated with family, faith, friends, health, location, education, travel, recreation, and free time. Previous generations believed that you worked from age eighteen to sixty-five, and then spent the last ten to fifteen years of your life attending to the other priorities.

With the following ingredients, you can cultivate an "elixir" of work and life, segueing easily from one to the other as the situation calls for it.

Organization	Determination
Discipline	Passion
Love of life	Optimism
Flexibility	Honesty
Self-esteem	Generosity

Using these attributes, fill in the sentences below to visualize how they integrate work and life.

Organization

✐ At work: _____

✐ In life: _____

Determination

✐ At work: _____

✐ In life: _____

Discipline

✐ At work: _____

✐ In life: _____

Passion

✐ At work: _____

✐ In life: _____

Love of Life

⟳ At work: _____

⟳ In life: _____

Optimism

⟳ At work: _____

⟳ In life: _____

Flexibility

⟳ At work: _____

⟳ In life: _____

Honesty

⟳ At work: _____

⟳ In life: _____

Self-Esteem

⟳ At work: _____

⟳ In life: _____

Generosity

⟳ At work: _____

⟳ In life: _____

Chapter 4

Personal Performance

In order for Performance-Driven Thinking to become a reality in our lives, it must begin at a personal level. In fact, personal Performance-Driven Thinking can be an even greater challenge, because there are no external standards to measure our performance. Personal Performance-Driven Thinking requires us to measure growth and success according to our own internal standards.

We all have personal areas in our lives that are important to each of us. They include: 1) personal health, 2) personal goals, 3) personal relationships, and 4) personal finance.

David L. Hancock & Bobby Kipper

___

*I*n some ways, our personal life is one of the most difficult areas to implement Performance-Driven Thinking. But it's also one of the simplest areas to supervise, reevaluate, and enforce it.

You face the task of defining what it looks like for you, because no one else can do that. But you also enjoy the privilege of absolute, dictatorial control over whether or not it takes root and does what it should. The world's response will help you determine how thorough and diligent you've been.

The Key to Performance-Driven Leadership

It might help to think of this chapter as the "gateway" to becoming the kind of Performance-Driven leader you long to see in shared human activities. Before you can be competent to lead others, you must first learn to lead yourself.

From this starting point, personal Performance-Driven Thinking can practically serve as a "leadership academy." There are no degrees, graduations, or alumni, because the learning never stops. In the course of time, the edge you display compared to conventional thinking will attract the right kind of people into following your lead.

Thinking is a spiritual, uniquely human quality—at the depth and detail we do it. The task we now face is taking an idea, a spiritual concept, and using our abilities with language to transpose it into a printed set of tactical, actionable steps. You have a basic blueprint of how this is done if you've received a basic education. Now, it is your turn to be your own "director of curriculum and education." You have to chart the course to your next level of maturity, intellect, and wisdom. So let's begin.

Your Personal Health

There hasn't been a more "health-conscious" time in human history, thanks to all our advances in understanding and treating sickness, disease, and injuries. But you've probably noticed that our "health-consciousness" hasn't made much of a dent in our society's unhealthful lifestyles. Without judgment, what habits can you think of that you've indulged in, or watched others indulge in, that diminish health? Here are some examples.

- Overeating or undereating
- Lack of exercise
- "Passive excess" (too much TV, video games, movies, social media)
- "Active excess" (overworking, extreme diets, too many extracurricular activities)
- Alcohol, tobacco, and drugs
- Unhealthy sexuality (pornography, casual sex/hookups, prostitution)
- Destructive thinking (pessimism, entitlement, envy, hatred, pride, or unforgiveness)

Performance-Driven Thinkers don't discount unhealthy psychological behavior. They're aware that the body and soul "talk to each other" and that what you feed into one affects the other. Spiritual lethargy gives birth to physical lethargy, and physical greed begets spiritual greed. Make a short list of any of these areas that are or have been difficult for you.

_____

_____

_____

_____

Your Personal Goals

You were meant to have goals in life, just like you were born to perform. Unfortunately, for the first eighteen or so years of your life, it's unlikely anyone taught you how to set them for yourself. They instead set them for you, and you either met, exceeded, or failed them.

But the fact that older adults are no longer setting goals for you doesn't mean goal setting itself should stop. It simply means you should now be the one doing it. In the space below, write out some goals in the following categories.

Faith:

_____

_____

_____

Family:

_____

_____

_____

Finances:

_____

_____

_____

Friendships:

_____

_____

_____

Fitness:

_____

_____

_____

In writing these goals, the acronym SMART (Specific, Measurable, Assignable, Relevant, Time-Based) can help you avoid unrealistic expectations. You wouldn't, for example, set a goal at age sixty of playing professional football.

Nor should you set vague goals like "be a better husband and father," because those are subjective, impersonal measurements from external sources. You can, however, *define* for yourself what it looks like to become better at relating to your wife and children.

Also remember—personal Performance-Driven goal setting is primarily directed at tasks and agendas that only you can accomplish or fail to accomplish. Corporate sales goals, for example, don't mix very well with personal Performance-Driven goals, because they rise and fall on the cooperation of external people—customers.

But you *can* set personal/professional goals to execute individual marketing and lead generation tasks that lead to sales. Nobody's in control of how many times you pick up the phone to make calls except for you. The math is obvious—the salesperson in cubicle A who makes 500 calls is likelier to have more sales conversations than the one in cubicle B who only makes 50 calls.

Your Personal Relationships

The old saying has it: "No matter where you go, there you are."

It's a simple way of saying that the common denominator in all your personal relationships—marriage, children, friends, extended family, acquaintances—is you.

Because relationships are subjective and involve other people, the optimal strategy to approach them is to predetermine how you'd like to be remembered by them. This will obviously "look" different for each relationship, but you can sketch some very broad, general categories.

In the table below, circle the words and phrases that you would like to hear your family and friends use when they describe you.

Close	Caring	Involved	Reliable
Fun	Wise	Helpful	Engaging
Knowledgeable	Secure	Powerful	Authoritative
Strong	Kind	Attentive	Intelligent
Thoughtful	Humorous	Memorable	Exceptional
Selfless	Considerate	Relaxed	Pleasant
Dynamic	Capable	Committed	Compassionate

Remember, there's how you *think* you come across, and then there's how others perceive you. This journey will involve being stretched and challenged, just like any other Performance-Driven model. The marriage and dating model is a good example of how quickly we rise to the occasion of improving ourselves to attract a mate—but somehow, we think we can forget about personal development once the wedding vows are exchanged.

There's also the reality that relationships change, over time, regarding what one person needs from another. Your teenage daughter won't need from you at seventeen what she needed at three. Your spouse will need something different from you after twenty years of marriage than they did when you were dating.

What *won't* change is the amount of effort and Performance-Driven Thinking you need to apply toward learning, adapting, and delivering what those relationships need at the various stages. You must be as diligent as you were presenting yourself as a single to the person who's since become your spouse. But what you present will most likely be different.

This is also true of friendships, relationships in business, and in your faith. Growth, maturity, expanded understanding, and appropriate responses are the most reliable factors in maintaining and reaping a great harvest from being connected. As the old saying goes, "Familiarity breeds contempt." Unless it's accompanied by consistent, meaningful, and energizing growth.

Your Personal Finance

One of the clearest indicators of Performance-Driven Thinking is personal finance. Unlike relationships, health, and goals, money directly correlates to how much thought you've given to performing in ways that communicate value to others.

If you want to know one of the biggest reasons that 97 percent of this world's money belongs to just three percent of its people, you have to understand how an overwhelming majority of those three percent *think*. It isn't a *better* or *worse* way; it's just different.

Financial freedom, and the ability to consistently make the right kind of decisions to build wealth, are hallmarks of a Performance-Driven Thinker. They are a rare breed in modern society, those who make decisions according to the resources they actually have rather than the ones they wish they had.

Take a moment to journal about your thoughts about money. How did you learn about it? What attitudes did your family have? For example, did you grow up being told rich people are evil and that money is bad?

Success as Temptation

Okay, let's be honest. Maybe you were raised to think money was evil, but that didn't stop you from dreaming about what you'd do if you actually got your hands on some. The risk of Performance-Driven Thinking is not failure, but success.

In other words, unless you have a built-in plan for *balance* when your Performance-Driven Thinking begins to pay off, watch out. Many successful people have shipwrecked in the name of "getting more" or "keeping up with the Joneses." One way to avoid this pitfall is to predetermine the five categories of work ahead of time and insist on an equitable division of your time among them.

In the table below, your task is to write down how you currently fill the five categories of work, and how many hours per week you devote to these activities. If you can only fill in one or two of them, that's fine, but to fully implement Performance-Driven Thinking, you should set a goal of *spreading* into all five.

Wage Work	Your job(s) and schedule:
Fee-Based Work	Your business and how many hours you spend in it:
Housework	Chores and household duties:
Study Work	Courses, certifications, reading, and study programs you take:
Volunteer Work	Work you perform for charities, your community, or your religious assembly:

If you own a business, you should tally up how many hours you spend performing your role and weigh it against your owner compensation. That will tell you how many hours you spend on it and what your hours are worth.

If you're deficient in one of these categories, it's usually because your time's being eaten by one of the others. Most often, it's paid work—your job or business—that gets in the way. The pathway to achieving balance, then, is to find adequate balance between paid and unpaid work.

(We should mention—some people's professions are in nonprofit work. That creates more capacity for workaholism, as evidenced by the huge degree of burnout in the volunteer and nonprofit worlds.)

Leisure Time

Don't forget, in all of this, that a life devoid of leisure is not Performance Driven. As a finite being with a limited lifespan and a daily requirement to sleep, you are an ebb-and-flow creature. Your balanced, Performance-Driven approach to life must allow you the freedom to rest and enjoy relationships with other people. Take a moment to write out some leisure activities you prefer, or perhaps some dream vacation destinations.

_____

_____

_____

_____

_____

_____

_____

_____

_____

_____

_____

_____

Leisure Time

Chapter 5

PERFORMANCE-DRIVEN BUSINESS

We are living in a time when people are just beginning to turn down promotions, quit the corporate rat race to start businesses for themselves, move to less stressful environments, and pursue less demanding careers. People are taking a new look at the meaning of success. They no longer automatically assume that the only way to be successful is to always be moving up the corporate ladder, to be burning the midnight oil.

An employee survey by Levi Strauss showed that 79 percent wanted more flexibility to set their own work schedules. "Presumably," says a personnel director, "so they can spend more time with their families and pursue other interests."

David L. Hancock & Bobby Kipper

What Shall It Profit?

Clearly, we made a cultural mistake in putting profit ahead of everything else, and the behavior of the modern labor force proves it. But is that poor understanding of business on the part of employees, or is it the failure of owners, stockholders, and executives?

One clear answer we have is in the performance of organizations voted into the top "Best Places to Work" over the last decade. The biggest corporate names in technology, such as Google, Amazon, Facebook, and Apple, consistently rank among them.

Do these companies report record profits every quarter? You bet they do, but it's not because they've found some magical pool of employees willing to sacrifice their lives for their employers' profit. So, what are they doing differently? We would say they're observing the Ten Steps of Performance-Driven Thinking in Business, found in *Performance-Driven Thinking*. Fill in the following blanks based on pages 58–59:

1. _____ your role

2. _____ your role

3. _____ your role

4. _____ workplace opportunities

5. _____ positive workplace relations

6. _____ questions

7. _____ opportunities

8. _____ from excuses

9. _____ and learn from top performers

10. Concentrate on _____, not systems

By using this approach, companies like these all over the world are able to turn their *entire staff* into leaders, instead of just having leaders at the very top.

It's difficult to be a top performer in an organization when totally disconnected from its mission and vision. The modern workforce success story is to get "buy-in" from as many stakeholders as possible, across all levels of work, for its mission and vision. The janitor, in other words, is as sold out as the CEO.

Performance-Driven Work

Inner job satisfaction comes when you discover work that ignites your passion and seize the opportunity to do it. This can sometimes include taking a cut in pay or a lesser role, because the money and seniority simply don't do it for you. In previous generations, such a mentality was unthinkable; today it's become quite common.

This matrix includes the qualities and environmental factors you should look for when considering a job or business—and that they should look for in you.

At work, Performance-Driven Thinkers:

Learn	Cooperate	Focus	Feel Passion
Delegate	Share	Respect time	Adapt
Plan	Manage	Market	Sell
Serve	Satisfy	Relate	Globalize
Improve	Perceive	Have a "cool" factor	Monetize

How to Position Yourself for Performance-Driven Work

There are three core principles you should keep in mind to position yourself for an economy that's completely shed its "low-price leader" mentality in favor of customized products and services for small, niched groups of consumers.

1. **Love your network**. In each setting where you work (remember the five types of work), you'll form connections and establish a reputation as a Performance-Driven Thinker. Because careers are seldom linear, it is critical that you cultivate a long string of people who like you to find your next project, position, or business opportunity. Below, make a list of the people you get/got along with best in your current and previous roles.

_____

_____

_____

_____

_____

_____

_____

_____

2. **What you earn depends on what you learn**. Next to who you know, your ability to segue from one skill to the next makes you more marketable, more often. That's not to say you should become a "jack of all trades, master of none." But it's clear that being a generalist is a precursor to being a specialist; the more applicable, marketable skills you have, the more

places you can get plugged in and build your network. Below, circle any of the modern economy's high-income skills that apply to you.

Creative writing	Graphic design	Software development
Copywriting	Public speaking	Digital marketing
Coaching/consulting	High-ticket sales	Investing/real estate

Of course, these aren't the *only* career paths you can follow, but they are the most lucrative that you can pursue independently as a freelancer or contractor.

3. **Care like crazy**. The old saying goes, "People don't care how much you know until they know how much you care," but that's a little vague. What do you care *about*? And how do you show that you care about it?

You will acquire a much better reputation as a practitioner by being obsessed with quality, satisfaction, and end-user experience. The market rightly grew fed up with subpar products and services, and the internet provided alternatives to the old, institutional businesses. Write below for a moment about things you can do professionally that you hate to see done poorly.

_____

_____

_____

_____

_____

_____

_____

_____

_____

_____

_____

_____

Chapter 6

PERFORMANCE-DRIVEN GIVING

One of the most pressing questions on the minds of people today is "How do I measure success?" Perhaps that's always been the case throughout history, but it's especially vital today since there are so many different ways to become financially successful. Money is not the ultimate measurement of success. Many of the world's most financially successful people agree.

As Jay Conrad Levinson and Jeannie Levinson wrote in *The Best of Guerrilla Marketing: Guerrilla Marketing Remix*, "Of all the pitfalls, the money morass is the deepest, darkest, and biggest. As lack of money is toxic to human existence, too much money can be equally toxic. That's why entrepreneurs like John D. Rockefeller and Bill Gates spent the first half of their lives accumulating money and the second half giving it away."

David L. Hancock & Bobby Kipper

Steve Jobs, the legendary founder of Apple Computers, is famous for never giving a dime to charity. Despite this, he achieved enormous wealth and influence. We mention this because we believe Jobs is an "exception that proves the rule"—an anomaly among most of the wealthiest people on the planet.

But Jobs's apparent stinginess would find much more company among average, middle-income people. Among people of modest means, there are many who believe one or more of the following lies about giving. Check any that you feel apply to you:

- ❏ I can't afford to give.
- ❏ Giving is a nice idea, but it doesn't help me in everyday life.
- ❏ You can be highly successful without giving.
- ❏ People around me don't give.
- ❏ Nobody has given to me.
- ❏ My giving doesn't make any difference.
- ❏ I don't know where to start.

We've found people most often come to these conclusions because of two great misunderstandings: the _____ and _____.

What Is Money?

In the space below, write down your definition of what money is.

_____

_____

_____

_____

_____

Where Do You Think Money Comes From?

Does money grow on trees? Fall out of the sky? Bubble up from the ground? Why is authentic money valuable, while counterfeit money is worthless? Jot your thoughts in the space below.

_____

_____

_____

_____

_____

If you've noticed, human beings are the only creatures on the planet who trade with one another. Two dogs who come upon a piece of meat will wrangle with each other for dominance. But two people with separate resources can, and often do, offer to exchange one for the other. Money is simply _____, a "certificate" that indicates you've supplied someone else with something they needed.

In the same way, we believe _____, because of a concept called "steward-ship." When you supply another human being with something they want or need, you *steward* the resources you have, in a good way. You care for another of God's children, and He rewards people who work in alignment with His other-centered, relational design of the universe.

Some people think being a "manager" or "steward" of God's resources means it all belongs to Him, and therefore, you don't get to do anything fun with it. But as the old saying goes, "Don't knock it until you've tried it." If you want to see people's faces light up, or watch them burst into tears of joy and relief, wrapping their arms around you for your generosity, learn the way of the steward!

The "3-R" Mindset of a Performance-Driven Giver

Performance-Driven Givers come with three built-in habits or lifestyle features. We encounter them every time we meet one, and we meet hundreds of them in our work with Habitat for Humanity (David) and the National Center for the Prevention of Community Violence (Bobby).

Reading. Performance-Driven Givers read at an abnormally high level. Check off the categories you read on a regular basis, and for the ones you don't, make a plan to focus some energy there!

- ❏ Fiction
- ❏ Biography
- ❏ Personal growth
- ❏ Finance
- ❏ Spiritual development
- ❏ Relationships
- ❏ Leadership

Write in the space below the titles of some of the most meaningful books you've read. You can use tools like Amazon's search to find other ones like them.

_____

_____

_____

_____

_____

Relating. Performance-Driven Givers get a lot of reinforcement by surrounding themselves and interacting with other generous people. Building relationships takes time and conscious effort, as well as a giver's mindset. But the good news is you don't need to reinvent the wheel. Many of the venues for building relationships are already built and at your fingertips.

Here are the three most direct routes to strong relationships based on giving and receiving, rather than buying and selling.

❏ Engage with givers on _____.

❏ Start or join a _____.

❏ _____other givers.

A few words about things like social media and business networking: There is always more than one way to network, and we are *not* encouraging destructive, negative behavior online, or self-centered networking. Before you engage in any of these relationship-building activities, you would be wise to define, in writing and ahead of time, what you *will* do and what you *will not* do.)

Remembering. It's amazing how quickly we forget that so much of the goodness in our lives comes from having great people in them! What Performance-Driven Giver *wouldn't* appreciate some expression of gratitude for their effort? Use the following three strategies to show other givers some love:

❏ Share and review other people's content or products/services
❏ Send gifts and handwritten cards
❏ Simply say "thank you"

If you've ever had any of these things done for you, it can't be difficult to imagine how the people you know would feel if you did it for them. Try it out, and see what results you get!

How to Determine if You're a Giver or a Taker

As we discussed, engaging in social media and business networking from a giver's mindset means you have to determine, ahead of time and in writing, who you choose to be. Most people who want to give can come up with a "to-do" list, such as identifying the right people and groups with which to partner. Considerably fewer people also create a "not-to-do" list that establishes ahead of time the people, groups, and behaviors they plan to avoid.

Below is a list of the 25 Qualities of Givers. Check off all that currently apply to you. On a separate sheet of paper, you should jot down the ones that don't yet describe you—and make a plan to work on them.

Givers:

❏ Enjoy their work
❏ Give personally to others

- ❏ Love the process of giving, not just the outcome
- ❏ Enjoy new challenges and opportunities
- ❏ Stay loyal to organizations they support
- ❏ Show concern for others
- ❏ Do more than is expected
- ❏ Learn continually
- ❏ Focus on goals
- ❏ Relate positively to co-workers
- ❏ Keep their personal financial life in order
- ❏ Deal with stress in healthy ways
- ❏ Have high degrees of emotional health
- ❏ Grow spiritually on a continuous trend
- ❏ Don't limit themselves to their comfort zone
- ❏ Don't overthink things; they take action
- ❏ Accept constructive feedback
- ❏ Show humility as well as confidence
- ❏ Listen to others well
- ❏ Volunteer for opportunities
- ❏ Connect people to each other
- ❏ Contribute to a positive culture
- ❏ Have a positive attitude
- ❏ Love to help others succeed
- ❏ Set realistic but attainable goals

If you can tick off all twenty-five of those, there's an excellent chance you won't spend much of your life worrying about any of the categories in Maslow's Hierarchy of Needs: physiological, safety, love and belonging, esteem, and self-actualization.

Most people still struggle with some aspects of being a taker versus a giver. Be honest: have you noticed any of the following characteristics in yourself?

Takers:

- ❏ Have cynical or negative attitudes
- ❏ Don't personally give to others
- ❏ Focus only on the outcome and not the process
- ❏ Avoid new challenges and opportunities
- ❏ Sow dissension in the group
- ❏ Gossip about others
- ❏ Only do the bare minimum
- ❏ Don't learn unless it's required
- ❏ Don't set or achieve goals

❑ Typically clash with co-workers
❑ Have untidy personal financial lives
❑ Deal with stress in unhealthy ways
❑ Lead emotionally unhealthy lives
❑ Stagnate spiritually
❑ Frequently display irritation
❑ Avoid people when possible
❑ Show no interest in personal growth
❑ Avoid things that make them uncomfortable
❑ Overanalyze and rarely take action
❑ Don't receive constructive feedback well
❑ Behave with arrogance and insecurity
❑ Do not listen well to others
❑ Do not volunteer for opportunities
❑ Care mainly about what they can get
❑ Rarely think about how to help others succeed

To become a Performance-Driven Giver, you have your work cut out for you. If you aren't growing in the qualities on the first list, and shrinking the ones on the second, there's hope. But it will take hard work and a lot of time to shift your mindset.

Quiz: Are You a Giver or a Taker?

Give yourself a score between 1 (low) and 5 (high) for the following questions to determine if you are a Giver or a Taker.

1. I personally give my time and money to help others in need.

   Score: _____

2. I give with a joyful spirit, not because I feel compelled or obligated.

   Score: _____

3. I constantly grow through reading, learning, and other personal development.

   Score: _____

4. I have a positive attitude and outlook.

   Score: _____

5. I understand the value of serving with a team and enjoy working with others.

   Score: _____

6. I see myself as a manager of my possessions, whom God entrusted with resources and opportunities.

    Score: _____

7. I grow spiritually through service, Bible reading, church involvement, and prayer.

    Score: _____

8. I have control over my personal finances; I keep a monthly budget and have low personal debt.

    Score: _____

9. I grow my personal income through a side business, investments, or other means.

    Score: _____

10. I maintain positive relationships with friends, family, clients, customers, and colleagues.

    Score: _____

11. I give to other business or community leaders by making referrals and introductions, and I often promote others' businesses.

    Score: _____

12. I genuinely listen to others with empathy and understanding.

    Score: _____

13. I volunteer for projects in my job or for service in the community.

    Score: _____

14. I set realistic but attainable goals, and I see them through.

    Score: _____

15. I strive to develop new habits that take my personal development to a higher level.

    Score: _____

16. I usually do more than is expected.

    Score: _____

17. I love to help other people succeed.

    Score: _____

18. I plan my personal, family or business giving in advance.

    Score: _____

19. I can accept constructive feedback and learn from it without taking it personally.

    Score: _____

20. I do my best to resolve conflicts with other people quickly.

    Score: _____

Total points: _____/100

Results

1–25: You need to do some work. But don't be discouraged; the vast majority of people are in the same category. A few rounds of the 3 R's of Performance-Driven Giving—Reading, Relating, and Remembering—should start to give you some ideas of where you can improve.

26–50: You're headed in the right direction. You've stopped making excuses, and you've started experimenting with generosity. Keep moving forward, and make time to examine your heart and ask why you want to grow. If you want to mature as a giver, your motives and values are paramount.

51–75: You're a giver on the edge of new, greater opportunities. The tests now shift, challenging you to rise the next level rather than remain at your current one. You have significant strength that can impact others at a high level.

76–100: You're at the very top of your game, where progress gets measured in millimeters of improvement. But don't get complacent! Keep seeking to become a world-class giver, and don't assume you can do it in isolation.

Chapter 7

PERFORMANCE-DRIVEN LEADERSHIP

With the rise of a new, more creative workforce, the expectations of organizational leadership have clearly shifted to performance. Leaders are driven to perform. Managers are driven to maintain. So leaders are not threatened by creativity the way managers might be. The "barking orders" mentality of top-down management is quickly being replaced with a performance-based model. This new leadership style is based on valuing a "let's work together" type of atmosphere. To put it simply, management is shifting to real leadership, and the "just do what I say" style is shifting to a leadership style that values performance for leaders as well as employees.

David L. Hancock & Bobby Kipper

Confusion-Driven Leadership

*I*t's happened to almost everyone under the sun—working for a leader who doesn't know what they're doing. The leader might be technically good at a skill, but that's not what leadership is; as tech executives know, computers and machines do what they're told every time. Leading *people* requires a completely different skillset.

From the groups and teams you've worked on, which leaders have misunderstood or ignored your strengths and aptitudes, or dismissed your ideas? What do you remember about them?

_____

_____

_____

_____

_____

A key indicator of poor leadership is when people get promoted based on skill in their current role, and not necessarily on their ability to teach and coach others in it. Have you ever seen someone promoted to management or executive level who had no business being there?

_____

_____

_____

_____

_____

Now it's time to play the game of trying to identify potential Performance-Driven Leaders.

Take a look at the current leaders you know, and write your observations about them according to the questions below:

Are they inwardly satisfied? Do they regularly display genuine confidence, happiness, optimism, and patience with others?

_____

_____

_____

_____

_____

Do they have a good balance between life and work? Workaholic leaders become slave drivers. Do the leaders you know say "Enough is enough," or do they ask you to stay late and try to squeeze productivity out of you?

_____

_____

_____

_____

_____

Are they a person of character? Are they morally compromised, ill-tempered, self-absorbed, sarcastic, and cynical—or simply unmotivated? Do they display "self-leadership" through a disciplined, focused, intentional life and attitude? Or are their actions random, chaotic, and unreliable?

_____

_____

_____

_____

_____

Do they enhance the success and profitability of the team? Your lowest-producing salesperson should probably not be the sales manager. Your third-string quarterback who throws interceptions and fumbles when sacked probably shouldn't play snaps in the regular season. Do the people you know in leadership *produce results*?

_____

_____

_____

_____

_____

Where Does Profit Rank?

Leaders who constantly beat the drum "sell, sell, sell" frequently operate from fear, greed, or both. But you will know a Performance-Driven Leader by the fact that they rank the importance of profit, winning, or being "number one" as less important than:

Their future	Their overall plan
Customers	Employees
Prospects	Families
Time	Inner satisfaction
Work-life mix	Balance

This doesn't mean profit or victories come dead last. Performance-Driven Leaders put profit ahead of:

Sales	Employee turnover
Response rate	Store traffic
Volume	Gross revenue
Press coverage	Ego
Status quo	Growth

How to Develop Performance-Driven Leadership

The big question for senior leaders is how to develop this kind of leader from their talent pool. It's like asking how you can duplicate yourself, being the owner or senior leader, so that the people underneath you think with the same degree of excellence as you when the moment comes and it's their turn to take the lead.

1. **Train all personnel in Performance-Driven Thinking**. Your team needs to read the book, and they need a journal like this to help them think through and develop Performance-Driven Thinking in their lives and roles.
2. **Train managers and leaders in Performance-Driven Leadership**. Synchronize their learning with those of the team, while adapting it to the duties and responsibilities of leadership. If your organization is a sports team, this would be the program for coaches, trainers, and team captains.

3. **Change leadership evaluations.** Describe your evaluation process in the space below, particularly if your teams are not returning the results or meeting the objectives you've set for them. Where does your current evaluation process fall short? What changes could you make so your leadership team adjusts their priorities, to inject performance into everything they do?

_____

_____

_____

_____

_____

_____

_____

_____

4. **Allow for constant employee feedback.** You could start with an informal conversation with several members of your team to hear how they perceive the transition to a performance-driven culture. Make notes on whatever they tell you here.

_____

_____

_____

_____

_____

_____

_____

_____

_____

Chapter 8

DEALING WITH NON-PERFORMERS

When people are rewarded for presence only and not performance, it creates an easy road that can have a negative impact on Performance-Driven Thinking. Many times, those who show initiative and creativity get looked at as problem individuals within the system. We discussed this line of thinking in chapter two, in the context of America's love affair with entitlement. Some of our job-related evaluation processes encourage non-performance. For individuals who choose to live out the philosophy of Performance-Driven Thinking, pursuing performance within this climate can become extremely frustrating.

David L. Hancock & Bobby Kipper

Performance Is Magnetic

Professional sports is full of stories from athletes leaving mediocre teams for the opportunity to play alongside legends. Although less publicized, the same thing happens in the worlds of business, nonprofit, and (especially) public service.

If you're a Performance-Driven Thinker, you won't want to stay in an environment that rewards non-performance. If you're in leadership, you won't retain top performers very long if you treat them equally to everyone else.

Elite teams, whether in sports, business, or elsewhere, attract top talent. They have their weaknesses—areas and roles that need experts. They never have difficulty filling them. They're likelier to have a waiting list and all kinds of leverage in selecting whom they place there.

Think of the top teams, companies, or organizations you've heard are very difficult to join. When Google, Apple, or Facebook advertise a job opening, how many applicants do you think they get? When teams with future Hall of Fame captains like Tom Brady or Peyton Manning need a new wide receiver, how many athletes would raise their hand? What does this tell you about the likelihood they have a surplus of Performance-Driven Thinking?

_____

_____

_____

_____

_____

Show Non-Performers the Difference

If we're all born to perform, then we should treat non-performers as though they really *are* performers. You do this by continually exposing them to the difference between the minimum wages of mediocrity and the vast sums afforded to top performers.

In a word, you reward winners while the losers watch. But you don't do this to shame them. Among those non-performers, you can actually motivate some of them if you begin to deploy the standards set by performers.

Values

If you know and can spell out your values, you can begin to set standards that "weed out" people who refuse to meet them. Write down your personal and/or organizational performance values, and make a habit of reviewing them. The more you have them memorized, the more you can dispassionately judge when someone is acting in or out of alignment with them.

_____

_____

_____

_____

_____

Work Ethic

Don't get tempted into the old interpretation of work ethic. It's not always about who works the hardest and the longest. It's about who works the most diligently at the fundamentals and details of their role until they develop such "muscle memory" for their job that they can do it in their sleep.

Strong organizations refuse to pile additional workloads on their members that are outside their job descriptions. Don't ask the first baseman to double as the outfielder, and don't ask the sales expert to keep handling account issues. Using this paradigm, how would you picture an environment that enhanced work ethic, either for yourself or the people who work under you?

_____

_____

_____

_____

_____

_____

_____

Delegation

The more you ascend in leadership, the fewer entry-level tasks you should perform. Performance-Driven Thinking usually "leads upward": you're likelier to get promoted or start your own enterprise. As you grow, you must learn to delegate tasks you should no longer do. But there are some important ground rules to follow as you do this. See pages 83–84 and fill in the following:

- ⏱ When you delegate, you double _____.

- ⏱ Unless a task is a _____, don't do it if you can delegate it.

- ⏱ The person you delegate to is responsible not only for work, but also for _____.

- ⏱ Don't delegate unless you're willing to _____ someone to do it with excellence.

- ⏱ Don't always tell people *how* you want something done. Talk about _____ more than process.

- ⏱ Be sure to delegate authority to make necessary _____ related to the task.

⏱ Tell the _____ about the tasks you're delegating to someone. Don't glamorize it if it's tedious or unpleasant.

⏱ The desired end result is that the person you delegate the task will do it _____ than you would.

Chapter 8

BELIEVING IN SMALL WINS

In a world where everyone measures wealth with money and success by obtaining the top position, anything less in many instances is not noticed or applauded. We are too busy celebrating big championships to notice that success happens in the everyday wins of progressive, positive performance. Our biggest opponent to the small wins theory is the current dominant culture. This opponent has caused many people to give up their goals and life's dreams. But we also participate in our own failure whenever we measure our success against that of other people and their current position or aspirations.

David L. Hancock & Bobby Kipper

How Championships Are Won

The Olympics, the Super Bowl, the World Series, the NBA Finals . . . they're exciting to watch. Elite athletes at the very pinnacle of their sport in elimination, winner-takes-all stakes. There's something about it that resonates deep within us.

Victories are cathartic for athletes, because they are the reward of a long season of hard work. For professional athletes, they're the reward for a lifetime of hard work. But for Performance-Driven Thinkers, they're an everyday occurrence, regardless of the final score.

How is this so? It depends mostly on you and your answers to the following questions.

1. If someone seeks to lose fifty pounds, is losing their first five pounds a victory?

(Y/N)

2. If someone needs to sell 100 units to make commission, are the first 20 they sell victories?

(Y/N)

3. If a failing student improves to becoming a passing student, but is not yet an "A" student, is it a victory?

(Y/N)

The sliding scale of the small wins theory is almost immeasurable. Because we're born to perform, it's very difficult for us to actually become "total losers." That's a very subjective (not to mention derisive) thing to say about anyone.

All or Nothing

Our culture's preoccupation with "newsworthy wins" rejects the spiritual significance of small wins. Sports "trash talk" is another example of this, which is one reason we don't recommend it. Take a moment to recount your "small wins" for today in the space below.

- Did you wake up early, or on time?
- Did you remember your essentials, like a morning routine, hygiene, and breakfast?
- Did you complete a successful commute to work, if you have one?
- Did you arrive early or on time for work?
- Have you maintained a steady, consistent pace throughout your day's work?

These activities have been minimized by our culture as "ordinary." To be sure, next to hang-gliding or climbing Mount Everest, they are very routine and predictable. We're just using them as examples here, because the average person is bombarded with the message that their daily lives are "nothing special" by our dominant (pop) culture all the time.

To understand the significance of these daily routines, you have to consider that there are people who woke up late, never slept, or are just now getting to sleep because they could only get work during the night.

There are people for whom hygiene and breakfasts are luxuries, and whose commutes involve five miles on foot to gather dirty water from unsanitary wells. It's unlikely they know what time of day it is, other than the position of the sun in the sky. They don't know whether their work is "significant" or not; life is a matter of merely subsisting and surviving one more day.

The point here is not to induce guilt for living in the advanced, prosperous West. We're only trying to get you to see it *inherently* as a win. Below, answer these questions about other "victories" you may take for granted.

✦ Did you travel anywhere in the past year by car, air, or train?

✦ Do you communicate, organize your day, and entertain yourself with a smartphone?

✦ Do you work and live in climate-controlled, insulated, ventilated buildings that aren't falling apart?

✦ Do you drink filtered, potable water and eat quality, inspected, and bacteria-free foods?

✦ Have you recently held your tongue, kept your temper, resisted temptation, faced a fear, or overcome adversity?

You could go down a long rabbit hole answering these questions. The point is to stop waiting for the news media to tell you when you're winning, and start proclaiming your own wins. Don't wait for your sports team to give you a temporary high when they win the championship. *Go out and claim your own victories.*

Chapter 9

Sustaining Performance-Driven Thinking

The key to sustaining performance in business and in life is effectively structuring your time—your most important asset. You've got to devote enough of it to your work so that you can earn a living and enough of it to your non-working activities so that you can enjoy your life. Performance-Driven Thinkers integrate life and work, but work does not take up all their life.

David L. Hancock & Bobby Kipper

Ten Steps to Bulletproof Your Performance Mentality

*I*t's time to do the deep work and fortify your foundation. You know you're born to perform. You know the obstacles of entitlement and everyone receiving trophies. You know that your attitude is central. You know Performance-Driven Thinking begins in your personal life, then in business, and then in leadership. You know how to deal with non-performers, and you know the value of small wins.

Now, let's codify this with the Ten Steps to Bulletproof Your Performance Mentality.

Step 1. You must start with *meaningful, achievable goals* for your personal and professional life. The mistake most people make, when setting goals, is aiming far too high. If we are stressed or over-worked, for example, we tend to think, "I need a month's vacation. Maybe I have to quit my job!" But your tired soul isn't the wisest person to answer this question.

Sit quietly, and start by visualizing what performance-driven success looks like for you, personally and professionally. Write it down, describing your vision in as much detail as possible.

_____

_____

_____

_____

_____

_____

_____

_____

In the space below, write some meaningful and achievable short-term goals that move you in the direction of that vision. Focus on the *outcome*. For example, if your vision is to win eight of the next ten games: "I will study film for no less than one hour after practice, and ninety minutes on off-days."

_____

_____

_____

_____

_____

_____

_____

_____

_____

_____

Step 2. Now you must *develop milestones in the process.* Using the small, achievable goals mentioned above, let's say a larger goal is to prepare your team for game day, by giving a class on your opponent's top five go-to plays. A good example of a milestone is when, in practice, your team can adapt quickly to alternate plays, so the opponents make the wrong moves defensively. Below, describe a milestone that confirm the progress and acceptance of your vision among your team.

_____

_____

_____

_____

_____

_____

_____

_____

Step 3. *Identify when you reach the milestones*, like a distance runner marking the halfway point of a marathon. If your milestone could be called "Ready to defend against Formation X," you also need to define how the *team* knows when they've reached the milestone. A good example might be, "During practice, we thwarted Formation X every time the practice squad ran it against our defensive front."

_____

_____

_____

_____

_____

_____

_____

_____

Step 4. To get to the next step, you must *chart your actions*. In a twist of irony, the celebration of reaching milestones has a short shelf life. As the leader, you're well aware that after a few tries, your opponent will figure out that Formation X doesn't work. At that point, they'll adapt and deploy Formation Y, and if that doesn't work, they'll try Formation Z. This is the hard part of leadership! No sooner do you create one milestone than you need to be busy creating the next one. But don't leave this to chance. If you're prepared for X and Y, but not Z, your opponent will have a field day running Z against you.

_____

_____

_____

_____

_____

_____

_____

Step 5. You might get stuck if you don't *identify multiple paths to reach your next milestone*. G.K. Chesterton once joked, "All roads lead to Rome, which is why most people never get there." You should plan and study how to do things ahead of time, but also accept that your best educated guess may be wrong. List below some alternate paths you can take to achieve your goals, and be prepared to resort to them if your preferred plan doesn't work.

_____

_____

_____

_____

_____

_____

_____

Step 6. You absolutely need to *surround yourself with positive influences to encourage you*. As Jim Rohn says, "You are the sum of the five people you hang around with the most." List your five closest friends below, and ask yourself whether they honor, encourage, and strengthen you. If they don't, you'll need to gradually introduce people who bring out the best in you.

_____

_____

_____

_____

_____

_____

_____

Step 7. Since we know that you are your own primary opponent when it comes to Performance-Driven Thinking, then you must *work through your own opposition* to overcome it. It would be a good idea to surround yourself with a mastermind group or some way of having other people hold you accountable for areas where you struggle. Part of realistic goal setting means writing down areas where you're vulnerable to quitting or giving up, and then allowing trusted advisors to ask you how you've handled these areas. Below, write down some of the internal thoughts or feelings you might experience when you become vulnerable to giving up.

_____

_____

_____

_____

_____

_____

_____

_____

Step 8. You have the same twenty-four hours in a day as the most successful people in the world. Both they and you are likely to run into situations where you say, "I don't have time to deal with this." But that's where the shared dilemma ends. For Performance-Driven Thinkers, things that interfere with their focus on performing are distractions. For the average person, it's the reverse—things that interfere with their distractions are usually opportunities to perform. Below, write down occasions when you get distracted or sidetracked. Keeping inventory of them is the only way to face the problem and begin to aggressively protect your time.

_____

_____

_____

_____

_____

_____

Step 9. You need at least one other set of eyes to *evaluate your process*. If you've ever attempted something where you *thought* you were doing it right and it still didn't work, you're using "too few brains." You need to engage more than one perspective to determine if your goals are realistic, and if they are, you'll also need extra eyes to review the steps you take to achieve them. Below, write down the names of a few friends, colleagues, or advisors you would trust to give you unbiased, honest feedback about your goals and actions.

_____

_____

_____

_____

_____

_____

Step 10. While approaching the finish line of your current goal, you need to be able to "pull back" and build vision for your next one. If you've achieved something, it won't be long before the celebration fades and you're left with the question, "Now what?" Performance-Driven Thinkers don't get fixated on one goal and forget about everything else. They're constantly looking up over the horizon, to determine what they should aim at next. Be careful not to let other dreams and goals go by the wayside. Write some of them down below.

_____

_____

_____

_____

_____

_____

_____

How to Structure Your Time

In the Performance-Driven Mastermind, one huge distinction we teach is between *efficiency* and *effectiveness*. It's great to be efficient with time, but not if you're "very productive at doing the wrong things."

Take a moment to list three to five activities you do in each of the categories below. These activities are the "big rocks" you need to build into your schedule, day after day, so that everything else gets built around them.

Self-Care Rest, retreat, personal development, etc.	**Goals** Personal, professional, spiritual, and physical
Profit-Generating Activities Income-generation, prospecting, selling, serving	**Family/Friends** Quality time, vacations, activities, recreation

Chapter 10

Selecting Your Stage to Perform

As Khalil Gibran said in *The Prophet*, "Work is love made visible, and if you cannot work with love, but only with distaste, it is better that you should leave your work and sit at the gate of the temple, and take alms of those who work with joy."

David L. Hancock & Bobby Kipper

Passion

What could you do late into the night, whether or not you got paid, long after everyone else has gone to sleep? What dominates your imagination, or has you gazing far off into the future? What sport, art, task, or expression could you do until the cows come home? Granted, there isn't always a suitable living attached to it, but we are creatures who have an innate desire to make a unique contribution to the world. Can you name yours? Write it down below.

_____

_____

_____

_____

_____

Challenge

The Romans used to say "*Virtus tentamine gaudet*," which translates as "Strength rejoices in the challenge." Have you ever come across a task or mission that was certainly not easy, but you loved the process of learning how to do it? People learn to ride unicycles and train for triathlons for this reason—to see if they can do it! Have you found work or hobbies that challenge you? Write them down below.

_____

_____

_____

_____

_____

_____

_____

Stretch

Your passions will keep your interest, and challenges will inspire you. But this is where many people stop, because you must find your stage in an environment that *stretches* you and forces you to grow. You might be a great collegiate athlete, for example. But not being selected for the professional leagues has ended many careers. There is always a higher level of dedication you can aspire to, and a daunting environment to go along with it. Below, write about an environment unique to your skills and abilities that would stretch you.

_____

_____

_____

_____

_____

_____

_____

_____

Support Systems

Some of the world's best individual competitors are quick to thank team-sized groups of people when they win at competitions. Parents, friends, family members, coaches, trainers, and advisors all have a hand in even the most solitary competitions. Who would you have surrounding you, supporting you, encouraging, and holding you accountable to perform?

_____

_____

_____

_____

_____

_____

Risk

It's normal to assess the risks of adopting Performance-Driven Thinking, especially in your professional life. Many people go from the safety of salaried employee work to entrepreneurship at great personal and financial risk. Those are important risks to assess, but there's another kind of risk—the risk of *not* pursuing performance. As we've noted elsewhere, the alternative is to remain in the dream world of entitlement and mediocrity. Write down some realities you might have to accept if you don't change your thinking.

_____

_____

_____

_____

_____

_____

_____

Performance-Driven Thinking about Your Stage

As you choose your stage and acclimate yourself to it, you'll face blind spots in your thinking. We're going to walk through some principles that will help you shine a light on common blind spots, and you'll have a chance to write down your own interpretation of what each one means.

Because we "think in language," as comedian George Carlin once observed, it's wise to write your thoughts out instead of keep them inside your head. Each of these principles will be "challenged" as you begin to perform, and you'll need the verbal residue from writing out what each one means to you. If you take this part seriously, you might even write these out on sticky notes or somewhere you can habitually see and remember them.

An example of what you could write for the first question below would be: "Anytime I start obsessing about money, bottom lines, or how I rank against competitors, I need to 'eject' and recompose myself."

1. **Recognize that the journey is the goal.** You must not become fixated on outcomes, to the extent you cannot appreciate your current position on the map.

_____

_____

_____

_____

_____

_____

2. **Achieve balance from the start**. You must not seek to "find" balance in work, relationships, leisure, or anything else. You must *bring* balance to them.

_____

_____

_____

_____

_____

_____

3. **Eliminate hurry**. The faster you do things, the more often you make mistakes. You are to become steady and diligent, but not *rushed*.

_____

_____

_____

_____

_____

_____

4. **View stress as a benchmark**. Like a sudden flash of pain from the body, you are to recognize stress as a warning beacon from the soul that you're in trouble.

_____

_____

_____

_____

_____

5. **Look forward to work**. Work is neither a right nor a curse; it is a privilege many people throughout the world would love to take off your shoulders. Retirement needs to be retired.

_____

_____

_____

_____

_____

_____

6. **No weaknesses.** Surround yourself with people whose strengths correspond to your weaknesses, and cultivate the kind of relationships that are very difficult to break.

_____

_____

_____

_____

_____

_____

7. **Become fusion oriented.** You must find ways to multiply your influence and impact by partnering with "allies." People, organizations, and businesses with a natural synergy with you and your mission are the strongest partners you can find to spread your message.

_____

_____

_____

_____

_____

_____

8. **Don't kid yourself.** Reality is still reality, and those who refuse its authority will pay a price. You have to place "checks and balances" against yourself throughout this journey.

_____

_____

_____

_____

_____

_____

9. **Live in the present.** You can *influence* the future, obviously, but you cannot control it. You can research and understand the past, but you cannot change it. The present is the only time you truly "possess."

_____

_____

_____

_____

_____

10. **Understand the precious nature of time**. You hate to waste your time, whether it belongs to you or anyone else. It is far more important to you than money.

_____

_____

_____

_____

_____

11. **Operate according to a plan**. A Performance-Driven life is not child's play. There's a written plan that charts your course, which you regularly review and revise to adapt to change.

_____

_____

_____

_____

_____

_____

12. **Be flexible**. Your plan is your guide, but it isn't your master. When things do change, you are among the first to accept it, adapt to it, and move on.

_____

_____

_____

_____

_____

_____

13. **Know that "more" doesn't necessarily equal "better."** If you grow and scale your mission and organization to reach the many, you'll only do it because of demand for the excellence you provide to the few. You're not chiefly aimed at "bigger, better, faster, more."

_____

_____

_____

_____

_____

_____

14. **Be interdependent**. A Performance-Driven Thinker is not a lone wolf. Your strength comes from "the many"—family, friends, customers, partners, suppliers, employees, mentors and associates.

_____

_____

_____

_____

_____

_____

15. **Engage in constant learning**. Unlike a seagull, which flies in endless circles until it finds food, you are geared toward constant learning and applying new, useful information and concepts.

_____

_____

_____

_____

_____

16. **Be passionate about your work**. You care about results, and not simply production, of your work. You want it to be impactful and life-changing for people. You demonstrate this through the energy and enthusiasm you bring to your work.

_____

_____

_____

_____

_____

17. **Focus on the goal**. Distractions will arise. What's the objective? Do you know where you're headed? If not, you'll end up somewhere else, as Yogi Berra once said.

_____

_____

_____

_____

_____

_____

18. **Be disciplined about the tasks at hand**. Anything you put on your schedule is a promise to yourself and others. Discipline will carry you through to the reward of completing it.

19. **Be well-organized at home and at work.** You bring order and efficiency to both environments, which enables you to last longer than others.

_____

_____

_____

_____

_____

20. **Maintain an upbeat attitude**. There's no room for pessimism or doom-and-gloom in your life. Problems arise, life is unfair, to err is human, and chaos and order are both normal. Regardless, you remain tirelessly upbeat and optimistic about your future.

_____

_____

_____

_____

_____

_____

Chapter 11

THE MOMENT OF TRUTH

Performance is not about sitting on the sidelines of life and work. Performance is about playing our roles to the best of our abilities and always looking to improve our performance. The old phrase "action speaks louder than words" truly defines Performance-Driven Thinking.

David L. Hancock & Bobby Kipper

Performer, or Bystander?

It's time to get clear about where you have embraced performance, and where you may still allow the bystander mentality to dominate. Let's begin by reviewing the qualities of each in the tables below.

Performers are

Self-starters	Self-disciplined	Self-guided	Detail-oriented	Responsible
Self-learners	Positive thinkers	Coachable	Task-oriented	Self-rewarded

Bystanders

Lack initiative	Resist feedback	Require guidance	Escape detail	Lack responsibility
Are easily distracted	Are quick to blame	Seek rewards	Procrastinate	Lack self-confidence

Now for your moment of truth. Circle "True" or "False" for the questions below.

1. I have a great deal of self-initiative.

True or False

2. I am usually the first one to start or complete a specific task or goal.

True or False

3. I constantly pay attention to the performance of those around me.

True or False

4. I get frustrated easily when others oppose my way of doing things.

True or False

5. I generally do not let the performance or lack of performance of others impact my activity.

True or False

6. In order for me to perform at my top level, I need personal or professional recognition.

True or False

7. I am not concerned when a task is left incomplete.

True or False

8. The impact of my personal or professional performance is not a major concern of mine.

True or False

9. The success of my day is not a direct result of my performance.

True or False

10. I do not have an issue with allowing those around me to outperform me.

True or False

Scoring

If your answers came out as follows, you are on the path of Performance-Driven Thinking.

1. True
2. True
3. True
4. False
5. False
6. False
7. False
8. False
9. False
10. False

If You Still Have Some Bystander Ways of Thinking . . .

There can be several reasons for this. We've usually that they all correspond to three big issues. Here are the ones you need to watch for:

Procrastination. We live in a time and culture where distractions and "alternatives" are everywhere. There's almost nothing you can't "put off until tomorrow," especially when it's not a high priority to you. The only way Performance-Driven Thinking will take root is when it matters more to you than circumstances or alternatives.

"Performance is someone else's job." Allowing others to take the lead in your personal and professional life will keep you in the bystander category. Performance can only happen when you step up and seize the reins of your life and work.

"No one notices me." Sorry, you can't just "mind your business" and keep a low profile because everyone else is too busy to notice your mediocrity or failure. The problem is that whatever you focus on, you tend to multiply. So if you focus on being lazy or self-indulgent in the shadows, sooner or later, you'll behave the same way in public, and someone will notice.

Make some notes here of scenarios where you could be tempted to procrastinate or shift responsibility for your performance onto others.

_____

_____

_____

_____

_____

_____

Maximizing Performance in Your Role

In the various roles you play—in your family, at work, in your community and so forth—you need to become the best version of yourself *in that role*. If you're a father, for example, it's no good trying to be "the best daughter you can be." That would be a huge disservice to your children.

Instead, using the information on pages 134–135, you must:

_____ your role

_____ your role

_____ your role

In the spaces below, write down the various roles you play at home, at work, in the community, and in other leadership positions. Then write about what it means to you to *know* your roles.

For example, using the father example, you *know* that it's your job to be responsible, mature, loving, kind, wise, firm, and instructive.

_____

_____

_____

_____

_____

Similarly, you'll do well to write down your *acceptance* of the privileges and responsibilities of your role.

Example: "My role as executive vice president gives me the authority to make large-scale decisions and hire and fire my managerial staff. My responsibilities are the success of my department and staff—to make us a productive, flourishing, connected place to work."

_____

_____

_____

_____

_____

Contrary to what you might think, it's also important to write out how you will <u>play</u> your role. Not "whether or not" you'll play it, but <u>how</u> you'll show up when you do. Performance-Driven Thinking does not consider "keeping options open"; you fully boughtin to the role, and your freedom is determined by how well you'll play it.

_____

_____

_____

_____

_____

_____

_____

_____

_____

Developing the Eight Performance-Driven Personality Traits

Chances are, even if you're becoming thoroughly performance driven in your thinking, you're going to have some work to do on your character and personality.

Studies of top performers all over the world confirm it, but here is just one study, an exhaustive ten-year audit from bestselling author and executive advisor Ron Carucci.

According to this study, among CEOs of large corporate firms, there is a 60 percent or greater failure rate overall. But what's interesting about that 60 percent who fail is that they're not what you'd call "simply awful." In the four subcategories of executive performance in Carucci's study, most of them perform well in two or three areas. But none of them could achieve at 80 percent or better in *all four*.

In other words, unless you hit "four out of four," the results do not change: you end up among the 60 percent failure crowd.

It's only when you can score 80 percent or better in all four categories that you enter the fold of the 40 percent who succeed.

That's a great analogy for the self-assessment you're about to do. The following eight personality traits are universal to all human beings. Not everyone can wield them at every level of performance. But everyone can wield them with constant self-improvement, so that they become the kind of performer who stands a chance of being elevated to the next level.

Patience

How would you rate your ability to "slow-play" situations, and work diligently at creating connection with people or excellence in a task? How much "runway" do you have to get your message heard in the marketplace before you run out of emotional energy?

_____

_____

_____

_____

_____

Imagination

What can you do with what you currently have? Many people get discouraged because they lack the resources to train, advertise, or get the kind of publicity that would lead to success, failing to see the thousand "small steps" successful people take to reach their goals.

_____

_____

_____

_____

_____

Sensitivity

How well do you listen to the needs of your marketplace or audience? Do you pay attention to circumstances, trends, attitudes, and competitors?

_____

_____

_____

_____

_____

Ego Strength

Unhealthy as pride can be, you also have to be able to weather indifference and not lose faith in your vision. Are you able to ignore the boredom and lack of appreciation of people close to you? Can you focus on pleasing your prospects and fans, even if no one else "gets it"?

_____

_____

_____

_____

_____

Aggressiveness

Are you willing to go the extra mile, financially or with time and effort, to reach the people you need to reach? Will you put yourself in the position to outspend and outperform your competitors?

_____

_____

_____

_____

_____

Constant Learning

Would you describe yourself as hungry to learn? If not, you're in trouble. Most people learn passively, like bystanders, just letting information come to them. You need to engage in *active* learning.

_____

_____

_____

_____

_____

Generosity

The expectation of the age is to receive some degree of information, knowledge, or expertise upfront for free. You can help prospects and customers reach a purchasing decision by giving them something actionable they can use, until they realize they need your professional expertise.

_____

_____

_____

_____

_____

_____

Action Oriented

Don't just read, listen, watch, and attend conferences and seminars. Take action on what you learn. Action is what transmits an idea in the invisible realm into a product or service in the visible one.

_____

_____

_____

_____

_____

_____

Chapter 12

The Stage Is Set—Now Introducing You

If we had been producing a movie, at this point you would hear the famous words, "Lights, camera, action!" During our journey toward Performance-Driven Thinking, we have covered a great deal of territory in our effort to convince you that your individual performance in life is a *choice*. We started this journey with the simple idea that you were born to perform. To enhance your ability to perform, we encouraged you to consider that to win in life, status quo thinking has to be a thing of the past. We then made the process simple by introducing the definition of Performance-Driven Thinking, which is the thought process that connects the desire to perform with the will to perform.

We explored how important Performance-Driven Thinking is in your personal life, specifically in your health, finances, and personal relationships. We then explored the idea of performance at work, and even embraced and promoted the idea of Performance-Driven Leadership. Finally, we shared with you various reasons why individuals find it easy not to perform—even providing a number of common excuses used every day. And throughout, we cast the vision of balance for Performance-Driven Thinking, emphasizing that the best performance occurs without stress, perfectionism, or workaholism. The journey is the goal!

We hope you have noticed there was nothing complex or complicated about Performance-Driven Thinking. While many people will view it as common sense, others will still find ways to escape the performance of a lifetime. So what about you? Where will you fall on the spectrum of performance? Will you simply read this journal and go on with a life accepting a destiny controlled by others? Or will you take the attitude of a new athlete or employee who has been recruited into a particular team or organization, intending to rise to the occasion and perform at a top level?

When considering our own thinking about performance, we are quickly reminded of various professional sports and their method of drafting players to individual teams. Each year sports players from all over the country work hard in hopes of earning the opportunity of a lifetime to play professional sports. These individuals did not become professional stars overnight. Every decision they have made in their personal and professional lives has been focused on helping them seize this opportunity. You don't win championships without developing, practicing, and advancing your skill level. This example may not resonate with those who are not involved in sports, but Performance-Driven Thinking and performance itself must no longer be reserved for the playing field.

To bring this closer to home as we end our journey, you must be convinced that the life you are living is much like a competitive playing field, and just like competitive athletes, your attitude toward performance will be the cornerstone of your success in your personal and professional life. The spectators in the stands are your family members, friends, and co-workers, who will be there to view your performance at home and at work. Your closest supporters are those whom you will hear cheer the loudest, but at the end of the day, when the applause is weak, performance still matters. At times in your life, you will feel like you are performing in an empty arena. You may not hear the roar of a crowd or the kind words of family or close friends on a daily basis, but remember that the stage is set, and the world is waiting to see your knowledge, skills, and abilities in action.

So why wait any longer? You control the lights on your stage. You control when the curtain goes up. You control when the performance of your life begins and ends. You are never too young or too old to embrace a level of performance. So the challenge is yours. Starting today, decide what you desire—and once and for all, go for the gold!

Five Steps to Performance-Driven Thinking

1. Realize you were born to perform.
2. Your education and life experiences have prepared you to perform.
3. Your knowledge, skills, and abilities are your tools to perform.
4. Establish what you want with clear goals.
5. Take willful action to achieve them by joining other performers at www.performancedrivenmastermind.com.

Don't Perform Alone

We all face a "fork in the road" for building a performance-driven life. Anyone who's ever raised a child will tell you: human beings don't naturally develop on their own. They need parents, siblings, grandparents, teachers, and a social circle of friends and acquaintances. Everyone you've ever met, in other words, is a product of thousands of interactions with people who shaped their lives—for better or worse.

Up until now, your life has been no different. You probably have people who care about you, like parents, perhaps a spouse, children, friends, or other relatives. You have people you work with every day who get to know you well. Maybe you're active in your community, or in shared activities like sports. There as well, you have a support network built around you.

But as you can probably guess, Performance-Driven Thinking doesn't usually pass from one person to the next through these kinds of interactions. If it did, we wouldn't have written the book. To the contrary, far too many people are *not* raised and educated this way. As a result, when they reach adulthood, they find life dissatisfying, painful, or out-and-out miserable. Loving and loyal as your family and friends may be, it's very unusual for people to inherit Performance-Driven Thinking.

That's why we've created **The Performance-Driven Mastermind**.

A curated group of like-minded people, pursuing personal and professional excellence based on the values, principles, and tactics we describe in *Performance-Driven Thinking*.

A culture of generous, authentic, highly motivated *allies*, deeply committed to succeeding by helping others succeed.

A fellowship of men and women who want to live transparent lives and go from making fear-driven decisions alone to performance-driven decisions together.

A council of trusted advisors who can look upon their own isolation, see it reflected in you, and lovingly tell you the truth when you lose focus.

You have to ask yourself if this kind of company is readily available among the people and places where you normally spend your time.

If it isn't, the follow-up question is simple: "When is that likely to change?"

It may never change . . . but if it does, it will most likely happen because *you* change it. You become part of the Performance-Driven Mastermind, and you bring your change back into your day-to-day life—and the people you know can see it in you. They can sense it, and they're drawn to it.

It will not happen, in other words, unless *you* take action.

Join us in **The Performance-Driven Mastermind** today at PerformanceDrivenMastermind.com.

ABOUT THE AUTHORS

David Hancock is a *Wall Street Journal* and *USA Today* bestselling author, the founder of Morgan James Publishing, and the co-founder of Performance Driven Thinking™. NASDAQ cites David as one of the world's most prestigious business leaders, and he is reported to be the future of publishing. As founder of Morgan James Publishing. David was also selected for *Fast Company* magazine's Fast 50 for his leadership, creative thinking, significant accomplishments, and significant impact on the industry over the next ten years.

David also serves as president of the executive board for Habitat for Humanity Peninsula and Greater Williamsburg, and chairman of the board of the National Center for the Prevention of Community Violence.

Bobby Kipper is a bestselling author, speaker, and coach, and the co-founder of Performance Driven Thinking™. He has spent over thirty years providing leadership development, training, and coaching to both the government and private sectors. Bobby believes that we were "born to perform," and his motivational style of speaking and coaching has taken thousands to their best performance to date. In addition, Bobby is the director of the National Center for the Prevention of Community Violence and is passionate about quality of life and human rights issues for all Americans. His programs to prevent and reduce violence have been featured by the White House, Congress, and thirty-five states across America.

A free ebook edition is available with the purchase of this book.

To claim your free ebook edition:
1. Visit MorganJamesBOGO.com
2. Sign your name CLEARLY in the space
3. Complete the form and submit a photo of the entire copyright page
4. You or your friend can download the ebook to your preferred device

Print & Digital Together Forever.

Snap a photo

Free ebook

Read anywhere

CPSIA information can be obtained
at www.ICGtesting.com
Printed in the USA
BVHW090948230321
603258BV00013B/229